The Power of Failed Ventures

Lessons Learned from Business Mistakes

HASSAN AFIFI

Hassan Afifi

THE POWER OF FAILED VENTURES
Lessons Learned from Business Mistakes

CONTENTS

INTRODUCTION – Embracing Failure as a Path to Success   v

CHAPTER I – The Fear of Failure: Overcoming the Stigma   1

CHAPTER II – Case Studies: Notable Business Failures &
Their Lessons   7

CHAPTER III – The Art of Failure Analysis: Extracting
Lessons from Mistakes   13

CHAPTER IV – The Role of Resilience: Bouncing Back from
Failure   19

CHAPTER V – Learning from The Past: Historical Business
Failures & Their Relevance Today   25

CHAPTER VI – Failure & Innovation: How Mistakes Drive
Progress   31

CHAPTER VII – Failure in Leadership: Mistakes Made by
Entrepreneurs & Executives   37

CHAPTER VIII – Turning Failure into Success: Stories of
Redemption & Comebacks   43

CHAPTER IX – Lessons for Future Entrepreneurs: Avoiding
Mistakes & Navigating Challenges   49

CONCLUSION – Embracing Failure as a Catalyst for Growth   55

About The Author   60

INTRODUCTION
Embracing Failure as a Path to Success

In a society that celebrates success and achievement, failure often carries a negative connotation. We are conditioned to fear failure and avoid it at all costs. However, what if we were to shift our perspective and see failure not as a source of shame and defeat, but as a powerful catalyst for growth and success? This book, "The Power of Failed Ventures: Lessons Learned from Business Mistakes," is a journey into the realm of failures, exploring their inherent value as invaluable learning experiences.

Our conventional notions of success often overlook the essential role that failures play in shaping individuals and organisations. We tend to celebrate triumphs, highlighting stories of unprecedented achievements and meteoric rises to success. Yet, lurking beneath these remarkable accomplishments are untold tales of setbacks, rejections, and mistakes that paved the way for eventual triumph.

This book aims to shed light on the transformative potential of failures in the context of business ventures. By embracing failure, entrepreneurs and aspiring business leaders can unlock a treasure trove of insights, strategies, and lessons that can shape their future endeavours and ultimately lead them towards greater successes.

Throughout the chapters that follow, we will

delve into the stories of entrepreneurs, innovators, and visionaries who have dared to take risks, only to stumble along the way. By examining notable business failures and analysing the reasons behind them, we will extract invaluable lessons that can inform and inspire our own journeys.

Moreover, we will explore the art of failure analysis, equipping readers with practical tools and frameworks to dissect and evaluate their own mistakes. We will encourage a mindset shift, fostering an environment where failures are not seen as indicators of inadequacy but as steppingstones towards improvement and resilience.

By embracing failure as an essential part of the entrepreneurial journey, we can navigate setbacks with courage and determination. We will discuss the role of resilience in bouncing back from failures, showcasing stories of individuals who harnessed their setbacks as fuel for greater achievements. These stories illustrate that failure is not the end, but rather a transformative turning point on the path to success.

In addition, we will explore historical business failures and draw parallels to contemporary challenges, revealing enduring lessons from the past. We will delve into the fascinating relationship between failure and innovation, uncovering how mistakes can spark creativity, challenge the status quo, and drive progress in unprecedented ways.

Leadership, too, will be examined through the lens of failure. We will discuss the mistakes made by entrepreneurs and executives, providing insights into the consequences of flawed decision-making and the vital importance of learning from these experiences.

The journey toward success is rarely a linear one. It often involves twists, turns, and unexpected detours. The individuals who have triumphed in the face of failure have understood the power of adaptation, perseverance, and continuous learning. We will showcase stories of redemption and comebacks, demonstrating that failure can be a step toward ultimate victory.

For aspiring entrepreneurs and those embarking on their own business ventures, this book will offer practical advice, actionable tips, and guidance on how to avoid common pitfalls and navigate the challenges that lie ahead. By leveraging the lessons gleaned from failures, they can chart a course towards their own remarkable achievements.

In conclusion, this book seeks to challenge the conventional wisdom surrounding failure. It urges readers to embrace failure as a path to success, to view setbacks as opportunities for growth, and to extract invaluable lessons from business mistakes. By embarking on this journey, we will uncover the untapped power of failures and discover the transformative potential they hold within.

I have gone through several failures before, so why should you?!

THE POWER OF FAILED VENTURES
Lessons Learned from Business Mistakes

CHAPTER I
THE FEAR OF FAILURE: OVERCOMING THE STIGMA

The entrepreneurial journey is often marked by uncertainties, risks, and the looming fear of failure. In the business world, failure carries a significant stigma that can discourage individuals from pursuing their dreams and taking calculated risks. However, it is essential to confront and overcome this fear in order to embrace failure as a valuable teacher and catalyst for growth. In this chapter, we will delve deeper into the fear of failure, explore its origins and impact, and highlight successful entrepreneurs who have not only overcome the stigma but also turned their failures into opportunities for success.

1. Understanding the Fear of Failure

The fear of failure is deeply ingrained in our societal conditioning. From an early age, we are taught to avoid making mistakes and strive for perfection.

THE POWER OF FAILED VENTURES
Lessons Learned from Business Mistakes

Failure is often associated with personal inadequacy and seen as something to be ashamed of. In the business world, where success is highly valued, the fear of failure can be particularly paralysing.

This fear stems from various factors, including the potential financial losses associated with business failures, the fear of judgment from others, and the uncertainty of the future. It can lead to a reluctance to take risks, an aversion to stepping out of one's comfort zone, and a preference for playing it safe. However, it is important to recognise that the fear of failure is a natural response, and it can be transformed into a positive force that drives personal and professional growth.

2. The Stigma of Failure in the Business World

Failure in the business world often carries a significant stigma. It is seen as a personal flaw or a reflection of incompetence. The fear of being labelled a failure can create a culture of risk aversion, where individuals are discouraged from taking bold steps, pursuing innovative ideas, or venturing into uncharted territories. This stigma inhibits creativity, stifles entrepreneurship, and hampers the potential for ground-breaking achievements.

To overcome the stigma associated with failure, it is essential to challenge the prevailing narrative and reframe our perception of failure. Failure should be viewed as a temporary setback, a valuable learning experience, and a steppingstone toward success. By changing our mindset and embracing failure as an essential part of the entrepreneurial journey, we can create an environment that fosters resilience, innovation, and growth.

3. Entrepreneurs who Embrace Failure and Find Success

One of the most powerful ways to overcome the fear of failure and dismantle the associated stigma is by examining the stories of successful entrepreneurs who have experienced failures and setbacks on their path to success. These individuals not only overcame the fear but also used their failures as transformative steppingstones toward greater achievements.

Elon Musk, the visionary entrepreneur behind companies like Tesla, SpaceX, and Neuralink, is known for his willingness to take bold risks. Despite encountering numerous failures and setbacks, Musk has persisted in pursuing his ambitious goals. From the failures of SpaceX's early rocket launches to the manufacturing challenges faced by Tesla, Musk has consistently learned from his mistakes and used them to fuel his determination and drive toward success.

Similarly, Oprah Winfrey, a media mogul, faced numerous obstacles and failures on her path to becoming one of the most influential personalities in the world. Early in her career, she was fired from a job as a television reporter and faced rejection in the industry. However, Winfrey persevered and transformed her setbacks into opportunities. Her resilience and ability to learn from failures propelled her to create an empire that includes television shows, magazines, and a successful media network.

Richard Branson, the founder of Virgin Group, is no stranger to failure. From failed business ventures to near bankruptcy, Branson has experienced his fair share of setbacks. However, he has consistently bounced back and turned his failures into triumphs. Branson's resilience, adaptability, and willingness to learn from his mistakes have played a crucial role in his entrepreneurial success.

These examples demonstrate that successful entrepreneurs do not view failure as a roadblock but as a necessary part of the entrepreneurial journey. They understand that failures provide valuable lessons, shape character, and refine strategies. By examining their experiences, we can gain inspiration and insight into how to overcome the fear of failure and embrace it as a bridge to success.

4. Strategies to Overcome the Fear of Failure

Overcoming the fear of failure requires a shift in mindset and the adoption of strategies that help individuals navigate the challenges and uncertainties of entrepreneurship. Here are a few approaches to consider:

- **Reframing Failure:** Instead of viewing failure as a personal flaw or a permanent setback, reframe it as an opportunity for growth and learning. Embrace the mindset that failure is not an endpoint but a step toward success.

- **Learning from Mistakes:** Take the time to analyse and learn from failures. Identify the factors that contributed to the failure, extract valuable lessons, and use that knowledge to refine strategies and make better decisions in the future.

- **Cultivating Resilience:** Building resilience is crucial in overcoming the fear of failure. Resilient individuals bounce back from setbacks, maintain a positive outlook, and persevere in the face of challenges. Cultivate resilience through practices such as self-reflection, self-care, and surrounding yourself with a supportive network.

- **Embracing a Growth Mindset:** Adopt a growth mindset, which emphasises the belief that intelligence and abilities can be developed through dedication and hard work. Embrace challenges, see them as opportunities for growth, and maintain a focus on continuous learning and improvement.

- **Seeking Support:** Surround yourself with a network of mentors, peers, and advisors who can provide guidance, support, and perspective. Sharing experiences and learning from others who have overcome similar challenges can help alleviate the fear of failure.

By implementing these strategies and adopting a mindset that embraces failure as an opportunity for growth, individuals can overcome the fear and stigma associated with failure and unlock their true entrepreneurial potential.

This chapter has explored the fear of failure, its impact in the business world, and the stories of successful entrepreneurs who have embraced failure as a catalyst for growth. By understanding the origins of the fear, challenging the prevailing narrative, and learning from the experiences of others, we can begin to shift our perspective on failure. In the following chapters, we will delve further into the lessons learned from business failures, provide practical tools and insights, and explore the transformative power of failure in the journey toward entrepreneurial success.

CHAPTER II
CASE STUDIES: NOTABLE BUSINESS FAILURES & THEIR LESSONS

*I*n this chapter, we will explore a selection of well-known business failures and delve into the valuable lessons they offer. By examining these case studies, we can gain a deeper understanding of the reasons behind their failures and extract key takeaways that can inform our own entrepreneurial endeavours.

1. Blockbuster: Failure to Adapt to Changing Times

Blockbuster, once a dominant force in the video rental industry, serves as a prime example of a company that failed to adapt to changing times. At its peak, Blockbuster had thousands of stores worldwide and was synonymous with movie rentals. However, the emergence of digital streaming and online rental services disrupted the industry, leaving Blockbuster unable to keep up with evolving consumer preferences.

Key Lesson: The importance of staying agile and embracing innovation. Blockbuster's downfall highlights the need for businesses to constantly adapt and anticipate changes in the market. Failing to embrace new technologies and shifting consumer behaviours can lead to irrelevance and ultimately, failure.

2. Kodak: Missed Opportunities in the Digital Age

Kodak, once a global leader in photography and imaging, encountered a significant failure as it failed to recognise and capitalise on the digital revolution. Despite being the company that invented the digital camera, Kodak hesitated to fully embrace digital technology, fearing it would cannibalise its film-based business. As a result, competitors seized the opportunity, and Kodak's market share rapidly declined.

Key Lesson: The importance of strategic foresight and the ability to disrupt oneself. Kodak's failure to seize the opportunities presented by the digital age highlights the need for businesses to constantly evaluate their strategies, challenge their own assumptions, and be willing to disrupt their existing models to stay ahead of the curve.

3. Nokia: Losing the Smartphone Battle

Nokia, once the leading mobile phone manufacturer, experienced a significant setback due to its failure to adapt to the rise of smartphones. Despite its early success in the mobile industry, Nokia struggled to keep pace with competitors like Apple and Samsung, who embraced the smartphone revolution. Nokia's insistence on sticking to its traditional mobile phone approach cost the company its market dominance.

Key Lesson: The importance of customer-centric innovation and continuous product evolution. Nokia's downfall demonstrates the need for businesses to stay attuned to customer preferences, anticipate market trends, and invest in innovation to meet evolving consumer demands.

4. MySpace: Failing to Sustain User Engagement

MySpace, the pioneer of social networking, experienced a rapid decline in popularity due to its failure to sustain user engagement. Once the leading social media platform, MySpace lost ground to Facebook, which offered a more intuitive and user-friendly experience. MySpace's cluttered interface, slow loading times, and lack of adaptability led to a mass exodus of users.

Key Lesson: The importance of user experience and adaptability. MySpace's downfall underscores the need for businesses to prioritise user experience, constantly enhance their platforms, and adapt to changing user preferences to maintain relevance in a competitive landscape.

5. Enron: Ethical Lapses and Financial Mismanagement

Enron, a global energy company, provides a cautionary tale of ethical lapses and financial mismanagement. The company's fraudulent accounting practices and deceptive financial reporting ultimately led to its collapse. Enron's failure not only affected its shareholders but also resulted in the dissolution of Arthur Andersen, one of the world's leading accounting firms.

Key Lesson: The importance of ethical practices and transparency. Enron's downfall serves as a stark reminder of the need for businesses to uphold ethical standards, maintain transparency in financial reporting, and prioritise the trust and confidence of stakeholders.

These case studies illustrate the diverse reasons behind business failures and offer valuable lessons for entrepreneurs. They highlight the significance of adaptability, strategic foresight, innovation, customer-centricity, user experience, and ethical practices. By examining these failures and understanding their root causes, we can learn from the mistakes of others and apply these lessons to our own entrepreneurial ventures.

In the following chapters, we will delve further into failure analysis methodologies, explore the role of resilience in navigating setbacks, and examine historical business failures to uncover timeless lessons that can guide us on the path to success.

THE POWER OF FAILED VENTURES
Lessons Learned from Business Mistakes

CHAPTER III
THE ART OF FAILURE ANALYSIS: EXTRACTING LESSONS FROM MISTAKES

F ailure analysis is a powerful tool that allows entrepreneurs to extract valuable lessons from their mistakes and use those insights to drive future success. In this chapter, we will delve into comprehensive methods, frameworks, and practical tools for conducting effective failure analysis. By adopting a systematic approach to analysing failures, entrepreneurs can gain a deeper understanding of the factors that led to their setbacks and make informed decisions to avoid repeating those mistakes.

1. The Value of Failure Analysis

Failure analysis serves as a crucial catalyst for growth and improvement. It goes beyond the surface-level acknowledgment of failure and delves into the underlying causes and patterns that contributed to it. Through failure analysis, entrepreneurs can:

- **Identify Root Causes:** Let's consider the example of a technology startup that failed to gain traction in the market despite developing an innovative product. Upon conducting a root cause analysis, it was discovered that inadequate market research was a significant factor contributing to the failure. The company failed to thoroughly understand customer needs and preferences, leading to a mismatch between the product features and market demand. By identifying this root cause, entrepreneurs can learn the importance of conducting thorough market research, gathering customer insights, and ensuring alignment with market needs before launching a product.

- **Learn Valuable Lessons:** Another example involves a retail business that faced a significant decline in sales and eventually closed down. By applying a SWOT analysis, it was revealed that the business had a weakness in its supply chain management, resulting in inconsistent inventory levels and delayed product deliveries. This weakness compromised customer satisfaction and led to a loss of competitive advantage. Through failure analysis, entrepreneurs can identify weaknesses like these, enabling them to strengthen their supply chain management, improve operational efficiency, and enhance customer experience.

- **Mitigate Future Risks:** Let's explore the example of a software development company that experienced a critical failure in the release of a new software application. By conducting a Failure Mode and Effects Analysis (FMEA), the company discovered that inadequate testing procedures and inadequate communication between development teams were the primary contributors to the failure. By recognising these failure modes, entrepreneurs can implement comprehensive testing protocols, improve communication channels, and ensure a smoother and more reliable software release process in the future.

2. Methods and Frameworks for Failure Analysis

a. **Root Cause Analysis:** Root cause analysis is a systematic method that involves identifying the underlying reasons for a failure by asking a series of "why" questions. Entrepreneurs can apply this method to delve deeper into the fundamental causes behind their failures and develop effective solutions to address them. By peeling back the layers of a failure, entrepreneurs can uncover not just the surface-level symptoms but also the core issues that led to the setback.

b. **SWOT Analysis**: SWOT analysis is a widely used framework for assessing a business's internal strengths and weaknesses, as well as external opportunities and threats. Entrepreneurs can conduct a SWOT analysis to gain a comprehensive understanding of their business's position in the market. By evaluating their strengths and weaknesses, entrepreneurs can capitalise on their competitive advantages and work on improving areas of weakness that may have contributed to their failures.

c. **Failure Mode and Effects Analysis (FMEA)**: FMEA is a structured approach used to identify and prioritise potential failures in a process, system, or product. By evaluating the severity, occurrence, and detectability of failure modes, entrepreneurs can proactively develop risk mitigation strategies. FMEA helps entrepreneurs anticipate and address potential failure points, reducing the likelihood of costly setbacks in the future.

3. Practical Tools for Evaluating Mistakes

In addition to the methods and frameworks mentioned above, entrepreneurs can utilise practical tools to evaluate their mistakes and derive meaningful insights:

a. **Retrospective Analysis:** Entrepreneurs can conduct retrospective analysis by reflecting on past failures and critically examining the events, decisions, and actions that led to them. This process allows for a deeper understanding of the context, factors, and influences that contributed to the failure. By analysing the sequence of events and decision-making processes, entrepreneurs can gain valuable insights and lessons for future decision-making.

b. **Feedback and Data Analysis:** Gathering feedback from customers, employees, and stakeholders is essential for evaluating mistakes. Entrepreneurs can analyse customer feedback, conduct surveys, and collect relevant data to identify areas of improvement and uncover patterns or trends that may have influenced the failure. Feedback and data analysis provide objective insights that can guide decision-making and help entrepreneurs make more informed choices.

c. **Continuous Improvement Frameworks:** Implementing continuous improvement frameworks, such as Kaizen or Six Sigma, fosters a culture of ongoing evaluation and refinement. These frameworks encourage entrepreneurs to continuously assess their processes, identify small failures or inefficiencies, and implement incremental changes to drive continuous improvement. By embracing a mindset of continuous learning and improvement, entrepreneurs can proactively address issues and optimise their operations.

By adopting these methods, frameworks, and practical tools, entrepreneurs can conduct effective failure analysis and extract valuable lessons from their mistakes. Embracing failure as an opportunity for growth and improvement, entrepreneurs can navigate future challenges with greater wisdom and resilience.

In the following chapters, we will explore the role of resilience in bouncing back from failure, discuss historical business failures and their relevance today, and examine the link between failure, innovation, and progress.

CHAPTER IV
THE ROLE OF RESILIENCE: BOUNCING BACK FROM FAILURE

Resilience is a crucial attribute for entrepreneurs when it comes to navigating setbacks and failures. In this chapter, we will delve into the importance of resilience and how it can empower entrepreneurs to bounce back from failure, learn from their experiences, and ultimately achieve greater success. Through inspiring stories of entrepreneurs who demonstrated remarkable resilience in the face of adversity, we will highlight the power of perseverance, adaptability, and a growth mindset.

1. The Importance of Resilience

Resilience is the ability to recover and adapt in the face of adversity. It enables entrepreneurs to maintain a positive mindset, overcome challenges, and keep moving forward despite setbacks. Here are some key reasons why resilience plays a vital role in the entrepreneurial journey:

a. **Learning from Failure:** Resilient entrepreneurs view failure as a learning opportunity rather than a final defeat. They embrace failure as a steppingstone to success and use setbacks as valuable lessons to improve their strategies and approaches.

For example, Colonel Sanders, the founder of Kentucky Fried Chicken (KFC), faced countless rejections and failures before finding success. He persevered through multiple business failures and kept refining his fried chicken recipe. Eventually, his resilience paid off, and KFC became a global fast-food chain.

b. **Overcoming Obstacles:** Entrepreneurship is filled with obstacles, such as market fluctuations, financial challenges, and unexpected hurdles. Resilient entrepreneurs have the mental and emotional strength to face these obstacles head-on, find creative solutions, and persevere in the pursuit of their goals.

A notable example is Howard Schultz, the founder of Starbucks. Schultz faced significant challenges when trying to scale the Starbucks brand and gain investor support. However, his resilience and determination enabled him to overcome these obstacles, secure funding, and build Starbucks into one of the most recognisable and successful coffee chains worldwide.

c. **Adapting to Change:** The business landscape is constantly evolving, and resilience allows entrepreneurs to adapt to change and embrace new opportunities. Resilient entrepreneurs are open to new ideas, flexible in their approach, and willing to adjust their strategies to align with changing market dynamics.

An inspiring example is Reed Hastings, the co-founder of Netflix. When the company initially started as a DVD rental-by-mail service, it faced the disruptive force of digital streaming. Instead of clinging to the old model, Hastings and his team embraced the changing landscape, transitioned to a streaming platform, and revolutionised the entertainment industry.

2. Stories of Resilient Entrepreneurs

a. Sara Blakely: Founder of Spanx

Sara Blakely faced numerous rejections and setbacks when trying to introduce her innovative shapewear product to the market. Despite the initial challenges, she remained resilient and persistent. Blakely's unwavering belief in her product eventually paid off, and Spanx became a global sensation, revolutionising the shapewear industry. Her story exemplifies the power of resilience in overcoming obstacles and turning failures into extraordinary successes.

b. Elon Musk: CEO of SpaceX and Tesla

Elon Musk, known for his ventures in SpaceX and Tesla, is no stranger to failure. Both companies faced numerous setbacks, including failed rocket launches and production challenges. However, Musk's resilience and unwavering determination allowed him to learn from these failures and make necessary adjustments. Today, SpaceX is at the forefront of space exploration, and Tesla is leading the electric vehicle revolution. Musk's story demonstrates how resilience can drive innovation and ultimately lead to ground-breaking success.

c. Oprah Winfrey: Media Mogul and Philanthropist

Oprah Winfrey's journey to success was marked by resilience in the face of adversity. She overcame a difficult childhood, setbacks in her early career, and professional challenges along the way. Winfrey's resilience, combined with her unwavering commitment to personal growth and empowerment, propelled her to become one of the most influential media figures of our time. Her story inspires entrepreneurs to embrace resilience as a driving force behind their own journeys.

3. Building Resilience

While some individuals naturally possess resilience, it is also a skill that can be developed and nurtured. Here are some strategies that entrepreneurs can employ to cultivate resilience:

a. **Cultivating a Growth Mindset:** Embracing a growth mindset allows entrepreneurs to view failures as opportunities for growth and learning. By recognising that their abilities and skills can be developed through dedication and effort, entrepreneurs can bounce back from failures with a renewed sense of determination.

b. **Seeking Support Networks:** Building a strong support network of mentors, peers, and like-minded individuals can provide invaluable guidance, encouragement, and perspective during challenging times. These networks can serve as a source of motivation and inspiration, helping entrepreneurs stay resilient and focused on their goals.

c. **Practicing Self-Care:** Resilience is closely tied to physical and mental well-being. Entrepreneurs should prioritise self-care activities such as exercise, meditation, and maintaining a healthy work-life balance. Taking care of oneself promotes emotional resilience and fosters the mental clarity needed to navigate setbacks effectively.

d. **Embracing Failure as a Learning Opportunity:** Resilient entrepreneurs reframe failure as an essential part of the entrepreneurial journey. They analyse their failures, extract valuable lessons, and apply those insights to future endeavours. By adopting this perspective, entrepreneurs can cultivate resilience and harness the power of failure to drive future success.

In conclusion, resilience is a fundamental trait that empowers entrepreneurs to navigate setbacks and failures. By cultivating resilience, entrepreneurs can overcome challenges, learn from their experiences, and ultimately achieve greater success. The stories of resilient entrepreneurs like Sara Blakely, Elon Musk, and Oprah Winfrey serve as inspiration and reminders that resilience can be the driving force behind remarkable achievements.

In the following chapters, we will explore historical business failures, discuss the link between failure and innovation, and provide practical lessons for future entrepreneurs to avoid mistakes and navigate challenges successfully.

CHAPTER V
LEARNING FROM THE PAST: HISTORICAL BUSINESS FAILURES & THEIR RELEVANCE TODAY

History has proven to be a valuable teacher, offering a wealth of lessons through the failures and triumphs of past business ventures. In this chapter, we will delve into the realm of historical business failures and explore their enduring lessons. By examining the mistakes and missteps of the past, we can draw parallels to contemporary business challenges and gain valuable insights to navigate the present and shape a successful future.

1. The Enduring Lessons of Historical Business Failures

a. **The Dotcom Bubble:** The dotcom bubble of the late 1990s and early 2000s serves as a cautionary tale of excessive speculation and overvaluation in the technology sector. Companies with little to no profit or sustainable business models were valued at astronomical levels, only to collapse when the bubble burst. The lesson here is the importance of sound fundamentals, sustainable growth, and a focus on long-term profitability rather than speculative hype.

b. **The Failure of Blockbuster:** Blockbuster, once a dominant force in the video rental industry, failed to adapt to the shifting landscape of digital streaming and fell into bankruptcy. The lesson from Blockbuster's downfall is the significance of embracing technological advancements, evolving with changing consumer preferences, and staying attuned to industry trends to remain relevant and competitive.

c. **The Decline of Kodak:** Kodak, a pioneering company in the photography industry, failed to capitalise on the digital revolution and the rise of digital cameras. Despite being the inventor of the digital camera technology, Kodak clung to its film-based business model, leading to its downfall. The lesson here is the importance of embracing innovation, staying ahead of technological disruptions, and being willing to disrupt one's own business to adapt to changing times.

d. The Financial Crisis of 2008: The financial crisis of 2008 exposed the dangers of excessive risk-taking, complex financial instruments, and lack of regulatory oversight. Financial institutions that engaged in risky practices and failed to adequately assess and manage their risks suffered severe consequences. The lesson from this crisis is the importance of responsible risk management, transparency, and robust governance practices to safeguard the stability and longevity of businesses.

2. Parallels to Contemporary Business Challenges

a. Technology Disruption: Just as companies failed to adapt to the digital revolution in the past, today's businesses face the challenge of technological disruption. The rise of artificial intelligence, automation, and the Internet of Things (IoT) is reshaping industries and business models. Lessons from historical failures teach us the need for agility, continuous innovation, and a willingness to embrace emerging technologies to stay competitive.

b. Market Saturation: Companies often face challenges in saturated markets where competition is fierce. Historical failures can provide insights into how businesses failed to differentiate themselves and lost their market share. Lessons from past failures emphasise the importance of unique value propositions, customer-centric approaches, and continuous differentiation to stand out in crowded marketplaces.

c. **Financial Stability:** The 2008 financial crisis highlighted the importance of financial stability and risk management. Today's businesses must learn from past failures and maintain robust financial practices, prudent risk assessment, and regulatory compliance to ensure long-term sustainability.

d. **Changing Consumer Preferences:** Consumer preferences and behaviours constantly evolve, presenting challenges to businesses. Lessons from historical failures underscore the need for market research, understanding consumer trends, and adapting products and services to meet changing demands. Businesses must remain customer-centric and responsive to evolving consumer preferences to stay relevant.

3. Examples of Lessons Learned from Historical Business Failures

a. **Nokia:** Nokia, once a global leader in the mobile phone industry, failed to recognise the significance of smartphones and the shift towards touchscreens and app ecosystems.

This failure to adapt led to the company's decline. The lesson here is the importance of being open to disruptive technologies, continuously innovating, and anticipating future trends.

b. **MySpace:** MySpace, a popular social networking platform in the early 2000s, lost its prominence to Facebook. MySpace's cluttered interface, lack of user-friendly features, and failure to cater to changing user preferences contributed to its downfall. The lesson is the importance of user experience, intuitive design, and agility in responding to user demands.

c. **BlackBerry:** BlackBerry, known for its secure and efficient communication devices, failed to anticipate the rise of touchscreen smartphones and the importance of app ecosystems. Its insistence on physical keyboards and resistance to change led to a decline in market share. The lesson here is the need for continuous innovation, adaptability, and a willingness to disrupt one's own business model.

d. **Xerox:** Xerox, a pioneer in photocopiers and document management, failed to capitalise on its innovations and neglected to develop a robust commercialisation strategy for its inventions. This allowed competitors to enter the market and erode Xerox's dominance. The lesson is the importance of effective commercialisation, strategic partnerships, and a proactive approach to intellectual property protection.

By studying historical business failures and drawing parallels to contemporary challenges, entrepreneurs and business leaders can gain valuable insights and avoid repeating past mistakes. The enduring lessons of the dotcom bubble, the failures of Blockbuster and Kodak, and the lessons from the 2008 financial crisis all emphasise the importance of adaptability, innovation, risk management, and customer-centricity. By learning from the past, businesses can chart a course for success in an ever-evolving business landscape.

In the next chapter, we will explore the connection between failure and innovation and examine how mistakes can drive progress and lead to breakthroughs.

CHAPTER VI

FAILURE & INNOVATION: HOW MISTAKES DRIVE PROGRESS

*I*n the pursuit of innovation, failure is not only inevitable but often a catalyst for progress. In this chapter, we will delve into the intricate relationship between failure, innovation, and progress. By exploring how failures can spark creativity and lead to breakthroughs, we will uncover the valuable lessons that entrepreneurs can draw upon to fuel their own journey of innovation.

1. The Mindset of Embracing Failure

a. **Redefining Failure:** Failure is commonly associated with negative connotations, but a paradigm shift is needed to view failure as a steppingstone towards innovation. Embracing failure as a natural and necessary part of the innovation process is crucial.

b. **A Culture of Psychological Safety:** Creating a culture that fosters psychological safety is vital for encouraging experimentation and risk-taking. When individuals feel safe to fail and are supported rather than punished for their mistakes, they are more likely to push boundaries and explore new ideas.

2. Failure as a Springboard for Creativity

a. **Embracing Iteration:** Failure often arises from attempting to bring new ideas to life. Through the iterative process of trial and error, each failure provides valuable feedback that guides subsequent improvements, ultimately leading to creative breakthroughs.

b. **Out-of-the-Box Thinking:** Failures challenge entrepreneurs to think outside the box and seek unconventional solutions. By embracing failures as opportunities for innovative thinking, entrepreneurs can uncover new perspectives and approaches that may have otherwise been overlooked.

3. Learning from Failures

a. **Fail Fast, Learn Faster:** Rapid experimentation and the ability to quickly identify and learn from failures is key to driving innovation. By adopting a fail-fast mindset, entrepreneurs can pivot, iterate, and refine their ideas based on real-world feedback.

b. **Post-Mortem Analysis:** Analysing failures through post-mortem assessments helps uncover valuable insights and lessons. Understanding the root causes of failures, identifying patterns, and documenting lessons learned creates a knowledge repository that informs future innovation.

4. Examples of Failures Driving Innovation

a. **WD-40:** WD-40, the ubiquitous household lubricant, derived its name from the fact that it took 40 attempts to create the successful water displacement formula. Each failure led to an iterative process that eventually resulted in a product with a wide range of applications.

b. **Dyson:** Sir James Dyson, the inventor of the Dyson vacuum cleaner, went through 5,126 prototypes and faced numerous failures before perfecting his bagless vacuum technology. His failures served as steppingstones to refine and innovate his design, leading to a breakthrough product.

c. **Google's Moonshot Projects:** Google's commitment to moonshot projects, ambitious endeavours that push the boundaries of technology, is built upon a culture that embraces failure as a learning opportunity. Projects like Google Glass and Google Wave may have experienced setbacks, but the lessons learned have fuelled innovation in other areas.

d. **SpaceX:** Elon Musk's SpaceX has experienced several setbacks and failures in its pursuit of space exploration. However, each failure has been met with perseverance, learning, and improvement. SpaceX's failures have led to groundbreaking advancements in rocket technology and have played a significant role in redefining the possibilities of space travel.

5. Overcoming the Fear of Failure

a. **Embracing a Growth Mindset:** Cultivating a growth mindset allows entrepreneurs to see failures as learning opportunities and fuels their resilience in the face of setbacks. It encourages continuous learning, adaptation, and the belief that abilities can be developed over time.

b. **Building a Supportive Environment:** Surrounding oneself with a network of mentors, peers, and advisors who understand the value of failure and provide encouragement and support is crucial. Such an environment nurtures risk-taking, fosters collaboration, and reinforces the notion that failure is not the end, but a steppingstone on the path to success.

Innovation and progress are often born out of

failures. By embracing failure as a springboard for creativity, cultivating a mindset that embraces iteration and out-of-the-box thinking, and learning from failures through rapid experimentation and post-mortem analysis, entrepreneurs can harness the power of failure to drive their journey of innovation. Through the examples of WD-40, Dyson, Google, and SpaceX, we have witnessed how failures have paved the way for groundbreaking advancements.

In the next chapter, we will explore failures in leadership, examining the mistakes made by entrepreneurs and executives and the consequences they can have on businesses.

THE POWER OF FAILED VENTURES
Lessons Learned from Business Mistakes

CHAPTER VII
FAILURE IN LEADERSHIP: MISTAKES MADE BY ENTREPRENEURS & EXECUTIVES

*L*eadership plays a pivotal role in the success or failure of any organisation. Effective leaders inspire their teams, drive innovation, and navigate challenges with resilience. However, when leaders make critical mistakes, the consequences can be detrimental to the organisation's growth and sustainability. In this chapter, we will explore failures in leadership that entrepreneurs and executives often encounter. By examining these failures in detail and providing in-depth examples, we will gain valuable insights into the importance of effective leadership and the lessons we can learn to avoid similar pitfalls.

1. Lack of Vision and Strategic Direction

a. **Failure to Establish a Compelling Vision:** When leaders fail to articulate a clear and inspiring vision for the organisation, it becomes challenging to align the efforts of the team and drive meaningful progress.

Example1: Eastman Kodak: Kodak's leaders failed to anticipate the shift from film to digital photography. They lacked the vision to recognise the emerging trends and adapt their strategies accordingly.

Example 2: Blockbuster: Blockbuster's leaders failed to recognise the potential of online streaming and focused instead on maintaining their brick-and-mortar stores. The lack of vision and failure to embrace emerging technologies led to Blockbuster's downfall.

b. **Lack of Strategic Direction:** Leaders must provide a clear roadmap for the organisation's future, outlining key goals and the strategies to achieve them.

2. Failure to Build and Empower a Strong Team

a. **Neglecting Team Building:** Leaders who fail to invest in building a strong and cohesive team limit the organization's potential for success.

Example 1: Theranos: Theranos faced allegations of misrepresenting the capabilities of its blood-testing technology. The company's founder, Elizabeth Holmes, focused on maintaining control rather than fostering collaboration and building a capable team. The lack of diverse perspectives and expertise contributed to the company's eventual collapse.

Example 2: Nokia: Nokia, once a leader in the mobile phone industry, failed to recognise the importance of software and the emerging smartphone market. The company's hierarchical structure hindered effective communication and collaboration, leading to missed opportunities and a loss of market share.

b. **Failure to Empower Employees:** Leaders must empower their team members, providing them with autonomy and opportunities for growth and development.

3. Poor Decision-Making and Risk Management

a. **Reckless Decision-Making:** Leaders who make poor decisions without considering the long-term implications put their organisations at risk.

Example 1: Financial Crisis of 2008: The financial crisis was partly attributed to the failure of financial institutions' leadership to assess and mitigate risks properly. Reckless lending practices and prioritizing short-term gains over long-term stability contributed to the severe economic downturn.

Example 2: Kodak: Kodak's leaders hesitated to disrupt their lucrative film business despite pioneering digital imaging technology. This failure in decision-making and risk management ultimately led to their decline.

b. **Ineffective Risk Management:** Leaders must establish robust risk management practices, identifying potential risks and developing contingency plans.

4. *Lack of Emotional Intelligence and Empathy*

a. **Lack of Emotional Intelligence:** Leaders who lack emotional intelligence struggle to understand and manage their own emotions and the emotions of others.

Example 1: Uber: Former Uber CEO Travis Kalanick's aggressive and abrasive behaviour toward employees created a toxic work environment and contributed to Uber's tarnished reputation.

Example 2: Enron: The leaders of Enron fostered a culture of greed and unethical behaviour, disregarding the impact of their actions on employees and stakeholders. The lack of empathy and ethical leadership ultimately led to the company's demise.

b. Absence of Empathy: Leaders must demonstrate empathy and understanding towards their team members, fostering a supportive and inclusive work environment.

Failures in leadership can have far-reaching consequences for organisations. By examining examples such as Eastman Kodak, Blockbuster, Theranos, Nokia, the financial crisis of 2008, Uber, and Enron, we gain valuable insights into the importance of effective leadership and the pitfalls to avoid. Leaders must establish a compelling vision, build and empower strong teams, make informed decisions, manage risks effectively, and demonstrate emotional intelligence and empathy.

By learning from these failures, we can cultivate the leadership skills necessary for guiding our organisations toward long-term success and positive impact.

THE POWER OF FAILED VENTURES
Lessons Learned from Business Mistakes

CHAPTER VIII
TURNING FAILURE INTO SUCCESS: STORIES OF REDEMPTION & COMEBACKS

Failure is not the end; it can be a stepping stone to greater success. In this chapter, we will explore inspiring stories of individuals who turned their failures into triumphs. These tales of redemption and comebacks serve as powerful reminders of the resilience and determination required to overcome setbacks. Through their experiences, we will uncover the importance of perseverance, adaptation, and continuous learning in the face of adversity. These individuals' stories demonstrate that failure is not a final destination but a transformative opportunity for growth and success.

1. Perseverance: The Key to Overcoming Failure

a. **Steve Jobs and Apple:** Steve Jobs, the co-founder of Apple Inc., experienced a significant setback when he was ousted from the company he helped create. However, he persevered and went on to found NeXT and Pixar Animation Studios. Eventually, Jobs returned to Apple and played a pivotal role in transforming it into one of the most valuable and innovative companies in the world.

b. **J.K. Rowling and Harry Potter:** J.K. Rowling, the author of the Harry Potter series, faced numerous rejections from publishers before finding success. Despite the setbacks, she persevered and kept refining her manuscript. Her perseverance paid off, and Harry Potter became a global phenomenon, making Rowling one of the most successful authors in history.

2. *Adaptation: Embracing Change and Innovation*

a. **Netflix's Evolution:** Netflix initially started as a DVD-by-mail rental service, but when the streaming revolution began, the company had to adapt to the changing landscape. Recognising the shift in consumer behaviour, Netflix transitioned into a streaming platform and revolutionised the entertainment industry. Their ability to adapt and embrace new technologies positioned them as a dominant player in the digital streaming market.

b. **Amazon's Diversification:** Amazon started as an online bookstore, but founder Jeff Bezos had a grander vision. The company continuously expanded its offerings, diversifying into various product categories and even venturing into cloud computing with Amazon Web Services. This adaptability and willingness to embrace new opportunities propelled Amazon to become one of the world's largest and most influential companies.

3. Continuous Learning: Turning Setbacks into Lessons

a. **Elon Musk and SpaceX:** Elon Musk, the visionary entrepreneur, faced numerous failures and setbacks throughout his career. When SpaceX experienced multiple rocket failures, rather than giving up, Musk and his team analysed the issues, learned from their mistakes, and iterated on their designs. This commitment to continuous learning led SpaceX to become a leading space exploration company, successfully launching and landing reusable rockets.

b. **Colonel Sanders and Kentucky Fried Chicken:** Colonel Harland Sanders, the founder of Kentucky Fried Chicken, faced repeated rejections when trying to sell his fried chicken recipe. Undeterred, he continued to refine his recipe and business approach.

Through perseverance and continuous learning, Sanders eventually found success, leading to the global success of the KFC brand.

4. Overcoming Personal Adversity: Rising Above Challenges

a. **Oprah Winfrey:** Oprah Winfrey, media mogul and philanthropist, faced numerous personal and professional challenges throughout her life. From a tumultuous childhood to professional setbacks, she used her experiences to fuel her determination and resilience. Today, she is not only one of the most influential women in the world but also an advocate for personal growth, empowerment, and creating positive change.

b. **Michael Jordan:** Considered one of the greatest basketball players of all time, Michael Jordan faced failure and setbacks early in his career. After being cut from his high school basketball team, Jordan used the experience as motivation to improve his skills and become one of the most dominant players in NBA history.

The stories of individuals who turned failure into success are powerful reminders of the human capacity to overcome adversity and achieve greatness. Through their perseverance, adaptation, and continuous learning, these individuals transformed setbacks into opportunities and created extraordinary accomplishments. Their journeys inspire us to embrace failure as a catalyst for growth, to never give up in the face of challenges, and to continuously evolve and learn from our experiences. By embodying these qualities, we can navigate the path to success, even in the face of failure.

THE POWER OF FAILED VENTURES
Lessons Learned from Business Mistakes

CHAPTER IX
LESSONS FOR FUTURE ENTREPRENEURS: AVOIDING MISTAKES & NAVIGATING CHALLENGES

For aspiring entrepreneurs, the journey to success is riddled with obstacles and uncertainties. However, by learning from the failures of others and gaining practical insights, they can navigate the entrepreneurial landscape more effectively. In this chapter, we provide valuable advice and actionable tips to help future entrepreneurs avoid common pitfalls and leverage failures for growth. By understanding the lessons learned from business mistakes, aspiring entrepreneurs can set themselves up for success and increase their chances of achieving their goals.

1. Setting a Strong Foundation

a. **Define Your Vision and Purpose:** Clarify your vision for your business and articulate your purpose. Having a clear sense of direction will guide your decisions and help you stay focused on your goals.

b. **Conduct Thorough Market Research:** Understand your target market, competitors, and industry trends. This knowledge will help you identify opportunities and make informed business decisions.

c. **Build a Strong Network:** Surround yourself with mentors, advisors, and like-minded entrepreneurs who can provide guidance, support, and valuable connections. Building a strong network can open doors to new opportunities and help you navigate challenges more effectively.

2. Developing a Resilient Mindset

a. **Embrace Failure as a Learning Opportunity:** Shift your perspective on failure and view it as a valuable teacher. Learn from your mistakes, adapt, and use failures as steppingstones towards success.

b. **Cultivate Resilience:** Entrepreneurship is a rollercoaster ride, and resilience is essential for navigating the inevitable ups and downs. Develop coping mechanisms, practice self-care, and seek support when needed to bounce back from setbacks.

c. **Maintain a Growth Mindset:** Embrace a mindset focused on continuous learning, improvement, and embracing challenges. Emphasise personal and professional growth and be open to feedback and new ideas.

3. Mitigating Risks and Making Informed Decisions

a. **Conduct Thorough Due Diligence:** Before making critical business decisions, gather all relevant information, assess potential risks, and consider the long-term implications. Take calculated risks, but always base them on a solid understanding of the situation.

b. **Build a Diverse Team:** Surround yourself with individuals who bring diverse perspectives, skills, and expertise. A diverse team can contribute fresh ideas, challenge assumptions, and enhance problem-solving capabilities.

c. **Test and Validate Your Ideas:** Before fully committing resources to an idea, test it in the market and gather feedback. Validate your assumptions, refine your product or service based on user input, and ensure market demand before scaling.

4. Effective Communication and Collaboration

a. **Develop Strong Communication Skills:** Effective communication is crucial for building relationships, pitching ideas, and inspiring others. Hone your communication skills, including active listening, persuasive storytelling, and clarity in conveying your message.

b. **Foster a Collaborative Culture:** Encourage collaboration, open dialogue, and the sharing of ideas within your team. Create an environment where everyone feels valued and empowered to contribute their unique insights and expertise.

c. **Build Strategic Partnerships:** Identify opportunities for strategic partnerships that can provide access to new markets, resources, or expertise. Collaborating with other businesses or individuals can accelerate your growth and mitigate potential challenges.

5. Continuously Learn and Adapt

a. **Embrace a Culture of Learning:** Encourage a mindset of continuous learning and improvement within your organisation. Invest in ongoing education, attend industry events, and stay updated on emerging trends and technologies.

b. **Seek Feedback and Iterate:** Actively seek feedback from customers, mentors, and your team. Use this feedback to iterate and improve your products, services, and business processes.

c. **Be Adaptable and Agile:** The business landscape is constantly evolving, so be willing to adapt your strategies, pivot when necessary, and seize new opportunities as they arise.

By incorporating these lessons and advice into their entrepreneurial journey, future entrepreneurs can avoid common mistakes and navigate challenges more effectively. Remember that failure is not the end but an opportunity to learn, grow, and ultimately achieve success. By leveraging the power of failed ventures and the lessons they offer, aspiring entrepreneurs can increase their chances of building successful businesses and making a positive impact in the world.

THE POWER OF FAILED VENTURES
Lessons Learned from Business Mistakes

CONCLUSION
Embracing Failure as a Catalyst for Growth

Throughout this book, we have explored the power of failed ventures and the invaluable lessons they offer. We have delved into various aspects of failure in the business world, from overcoming the fear and stigma associated with it to analysing notable business failures, extracting lessons, and understanding the role of resilience, historical failures, innovation, leadership mistakes, redemption stories, and practical advice for future entrepreneurs. Now, as we conclude this journey, let us recap the key themes and takeaways that can guide us on our entrepreneurial path.

One of the fundamental insights we have uncovered is that failures are not setbacks but steppingstones toward success. Each failure presents an opportunity for growth, learning, and adaptation. By embracing failure, we cultivate resilience, develop a growth mindset, and discover our true capabilities.

We have seen the importance of facing the fear of failure head-on. The stigma attached to failure often paralyses individuals and hinders their entrepreneurial aspirations. However, by understanding that failure is a natural part of the entrepreneurial journey, we can overcome this fear and seize opportunities with confidence.

The examination of notable business failures has shown us that even the most successful entrepreneurs have faced setbacks. Their stories teach us that failure is not an indication of incompetence but a springboard for future success. By embracing our failures, we can learn from them, pivot our strategies, and uncover new pathways to achieving our goals.

Failure analysis has emerged as a powerful tool for extracting lessons from mistakes. By employing effective methods and frameworks, we can dissect our failures, identify the underlying causes, and gain valuable insights. This analytical approach enables us to make informed decisions, mitigate risks, and set ourselves up for success.

Resilience has proven to be a crucial trait in navigating setbacks and failures. The stories of entrepreneurs who have demonstrated unwavering determination and perseverance inspire us to push through challenges and keep moving forward. Resilience enables us to bounce back from failures, adapt to changing circumstances, and ultimately achieve greater success.

The exploration of historical business failures has provided us with enduring lessons. By drawing parallels between past failures and contemporary challenges, we gain insights into the cyclical nature of business and the common pitfalls to avoid. History serves as a valuable teacher, reminding us of the mistakes made by others and guiding us toward more informed decision-making.

Innovation has emerged as a key driver of progress, and failures often pave the way for breakthroughs. By embracing experimentation, taking calculated risks, and learning from our failures, we can foster an environment conducive to innovation. Failures spark creativity, challenge the status quo, and inspire us to think outside the box.

Leadership failures have highlighted the critical role of effective leadership in business success. By recognising the common mistakes made by entrepreneurs and executives, we can cultivate the qualities of effective leadership, such as clear communication, sound decision-making, and fostering a positive and collaborative work culture. Leadership failures remind us of the impact our actions and decisions have on the overall success of our ventures.

The stories of individuals who have turned failure into success inspire us to persevere in the face of adversity. These tales of redemption teach us the importance of continuous learning, adaptation, and a resilient mindset. They remind us that failure does not define us but how we respond to it shapes our future.

THE POWER OF FAILED VENTURES
Lessons Learned from Business Mistakes

As we conclude this book, I encourage you to embrace failure as an essential part of your entrepreneurial journey. Recognise that failures are not defeats but opportunities for growth and improvement. Embrace the lessons learned from business mistakes and apply them to your own ventures. Cultivate resilience, develop a growth mindset, and never be afraid to take calculated risks.

Remember that success is not a linear path but a series of failures, learnings, and triumphs. By embracing failure as a catalyst for growth, you position yourself to create meaningful and impactful ventures. So, step forward with confidence, learn from your mistakes, and let failures propel you toward the heights of entrepreneurial success.

Best of luck on your journey!

Hassan Afifi

ABOUT THE AUTHOR

Hassan Afifi is a UK-based investment professional. He started investing and trading in financial markets in the early 1990s while at university. He holds a BA in economics.

Hassan has worked in institutional equity sales, advising some of the world's largest fund managers on their investments across different geographies and sectors.

He has also worked in corporate finance, helping entrepreneurs start or grow their businesses, raise funds for their projects, and guide management teams through their financial planning processes.

Hassan returned to the investment world full-time in 2020 focusing on wealth management to try and help as many people as he can to achieve their financial freedom.